Sacagawea

1788–1812

by Rosemary Wallner

Content Consultant:
Melodie Andrews
Associate Professor of Early American History
Minnesota State University, Mankato

Blue Earth Books

an imprint of Capstone Press
Mankato, Minnesota

Blue Earth Books are published by Capstone Press
151 Good Counsel Drive, P.O. Box 669, Mankato, Minnesota 56002
http://www.capstone-press.com

Library of Congress Cataloging-in-Publication Data
Wallner, Rosemary, 1964–
  Sacagawea, 1788–1812.
  p. cm.—(American Indian biographies)
  Summary: A biography of Sacagawea, the Shoshoni who was an interpreter on the Lewis and Clark
Expedition, including her childhood in a Shoshoni village, capture by Hidatsas, and reunion with her
brother. Includes sidebars, activities, a chronology, and a map.
  Includes bibliographical references and index.
  ISBN 0-7368-1213-X (hardcover)
  1. Sacagawea, 1786–1884—Juvenile literature. 2. Lewis and Clark Expedition (1804–1806)—Juvenile
literature. 3. Shoshoni women—Biography—Juvenile literature. 4. Shoshoni Indians—Biography—Juvenile
literature. 5. Sacagawea, 1786–1884—Childhood and youth—Juvenile literature. [1. Sacagawea,
1786–1884. 2. Lewis and Clark Expedition (1804–1806) 3. Shoshoni Indians—Biography. 4. Indians of
North America—Biography. 5. Women—Biography.] I. Title. II. Series
  F592.7.S123 W35 2003
  978.004'9745—dc21   2001008088

Editorial Credits
Editors: Rachel Koestler-Grack and
    Katy Kudela
Cover Designer: Heather Kindseth
Interior Layout Designers: Jennifer
    Schonborn and Heather Kindseth
Interior Illustrator: Jennifer Schonborn
Production Designers: Jennifer
    Schonborn and Gene Bentdahl
Photo Researcher: Mary Englar

Photo Credits
Michael Haynes, cover, 17, 28, 29 (both top); Capstone
Press Archives, cover (glass beads); Amon Carter Museum,
4–5; CORBIS, 8–9; Art Resource, 10, 14–15; Capstone
Press/Gary Sundermeyer, 11; Courtesy of Mrs. Clymer and
the Clymer Museum of Art, 12–13, 18–19, 24–25, 26–27;
Coeur D'Alene Galleries, 20; Art Museum of Missoula, 21;
Jefferson National Expansion Memorial, 22–23, 29 (bottom)

Editors' Note:
People disagree on the spelling of Sacagawea's
name. Most people use the spelling Sacagawea.
Some use Sakakawea. Both of these spellings are
English spellings of the Hidatsa language. Others
use the spelling Sacajawea.

1 2 3 4 5 6 07 06 05 04 03 02

Contents

CHAPTER 1

An Important Rescue

When other tribes saw Sacagawea with the explorers, they knew the group was not a war party.

By the time Sacagawea [Sah-cah-gah-WEE-ah] was 17 years old, she already had experienced more adventures than most young Lemhi Shoshone women her age. She had been taken captive by a group of Hidatsa Indian warriors when she was 12 years old. She lived in a Hidatsa village and later was purchased by a French fur trader named Toussaint Charbonneau, who took her as a wife.

In November 1804, Sacagawea met two white explorers who visited the Hidatsa village. They were Meriwether Lewis and William Clark. They told the Hidatsa that they were on a peaceful exploration of the West.

The explorers traveled with a group of 31 men and a big dog. The men built a winter shelter near the Hidatsa village. During the winter, Charbonneau took Sacagawea to the white men's shelter. While there, Sacagawea had a baby son. She named him Pomp.

As the weather became warmer, the white explorers packed supplies and food, preparing for their journey. Sacagawea learned that she and Charbonneau would be traveling with Lewis and Clark. They needed her to speak Shoshone to her people when they traveled through her homeland. On April 7, Sacagawea securely wrapped baby Pomp in his cradleboard and strapped the cradleboard to her back. She then joined Charbonneau on the banks of the Missouri River near the Hidatsa village.

BITTERROOT
MOUNTAINS

Great Falls

Hidatsa
Village

Fort
Clatsop

ROCKY MOUNTAINS

Lemhi
Camp

Fort Manuel

Missouri River

St. Louis,
Missouri

Day after day, the group traveled by boat on the Missouri River. Sacagawea sat quietly in one of the long, narrow boats, with 3-month-old Pomp on her lap. Charbonneau guided the boat with the sail.

Charbonneau moved the sail to adjust for the wind. He may have accidentally pushed the sail in the wrong direction, causing the boat to tip. Men in the boat fumbled about trying to keep the boat from turning upside down.

Water quickly filled the bottom of the boat. Many of the men were scared. Charbonneau could not swim and was frightened. Sacagawea saw the fear in the men's eyes as they tried to steady the boat. She knew how to swim well and was not afraid.

Some of the supplies washed out of the boat and into the river. The explorers' precious papers and compass floated on the surface. Sacagawea calmly grabbed the items out of the water before they sank.

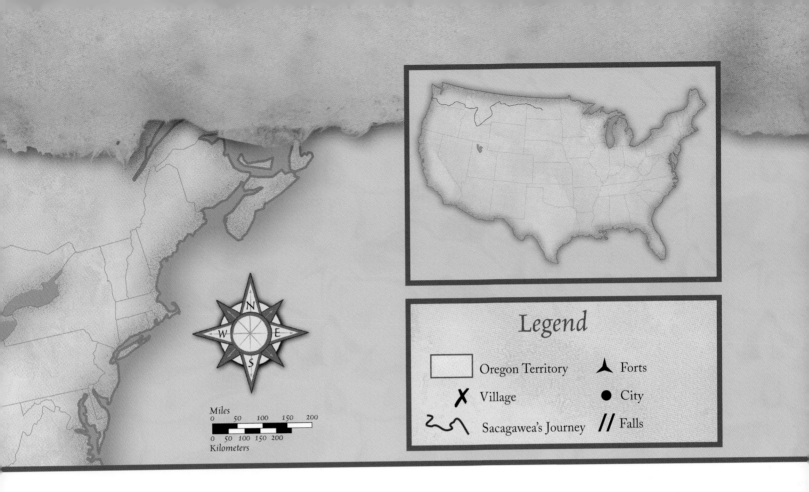

Lewis and Clark were grateful to Sacagawea for rescuing their things. Without the compass, the explorers would have had trouble navigating their direction. The papers contained maps and important notes about the group's discoveries.

Throughout the journey with Lewis and Clark, Sacagawea proved to be a valuable member of the group. She showed the men which wild foods were good to eat and which plants could be used for medicine. She served as a symbol of peace to other American Indian tribes. When American Indians saw that the group of explorers was traveling with a woman and a small child, they knew the group was not a war party.

Today, people remember Sacagawea for her strength and courage. She aided peace among different nations. Sacagawea is also remembered for her contributions to the Lewis and Clark Expedition. People have built several monuments to preserve her memory.

CHAPTER 2

Capture on the Jefferson River

The Lemhi Shoshone camped near mountain rivers.

In 1788, Sacagawea was born in a Lemhi Shoshone encampment near present-day Salmon, Idaho. Sacagawea's father was the tribal chief. She had an older brother named Cameahwait, a younger brother named Snag, and an older sister named Pine Girl.

The Lemhi Shoshone were nomadic. Sacagawea's people often moved from place to place. They followed elk, deer, or buffalo herds and the salmon runs in the rivers of east-central Idaho.

When Sacagawea was 12 years old, her people camped near the Jefferson River by present-day Three Forks, Montana. Her people were on a buffalo hunt. Sacagawea stayed with her family while most of the men in the camp rode onto the plains to make the buffalo kills. The hunters killed the buffalo and then came back to get the women, who helped cut the meat and prepare the skins.

Sacagawea helped move back to the Salmon River area. It had been a long time since she enjoyed walking along the rocky shores of the Salmon River. She and her friend, Mountain Sage, often ate freshly picked ripe chokecherries, gooseberries, and currants.

Early one morning, Sacagawea's brother gathered his bow, arrows, and knife. Cameahwait was going on one of his first buffalo hunts with the other men.

Sacagawea got up from her bed and put her hand on Cameahwait's shoulder. "Be careful, brother," she whispered. "There are many bad spirits on these plains."

"Do not worry, Sacagawea," he replied. "Tonight you will have many buffalo skins to scrape." He kissed her cheek and walked out of the tepee.

After the hunters left for the plains, Sacagawea walked past the morning fire that burned in the center of camp. Buffalo skins hung drying over nearby branches. She stopped outside Mountain Sage's tepee.

Mountain Sage peeked out from behind the thick elk-skin door flap. "I heard your footsteps," she whispered. Mountain Sage climbed out of the tepee and took Sacagawea's hands. The two girls huddled in the shadows beside the tepee.

A loud shriek suddenly broke the peaceful morning. "Hidatsa warriors!" Sacagawea shouted. Her body went stiff with fear.

Shoshone women helped to water the horses.

The Hidatsa Indians were an enemy tribe of the Lemhi Shoshone and often stole horses from Sacagawea's tribe.

One of the few men in camp rushed out of his tepee, calling to the others. His warning cries stopped suddenly as an arrow pierced his heart. Women and children fled into the nearby forest.

Gooseberry Cobbler

What You Need

Ingredients

2 cups (500 mL) all-purpose flour

½ teaspoon (2 mL) baking powder

½ teaspoon (2 mL) salt

½ cup (125 mL) cornmeal

¾ cup (175 mL) butter

¾ cup (175 mL) boiling water

1 tablespoon (15 mL) butter, for greasing

2 tablespoons (30 mL) cornmeal, divided

2 15-ounce (425-gram) cans sweetened, whole gooseberries

1 teaspoon (5 mL) honey

1 teaspoon (5 mL) lemon juice

Equipment

2 medium-sized mixing bowls

fork

dry-ingredient measuring cups

liquid measuring cup

pan to boil water

paper towel

wooden spoon

measuring spoons

potato masher

What You Do

1. Preheat over to 425°F (218°C).
2. Mix flour, baking powder, salt, and ½ cup (125 mL) of cornmeal in a medium-sized bowl.
3. Drop ¾ cup (175 mL) of butter into flour mixture. Using a fork, mix butter into flour mixture until the mixture is in small, pea-sized pieces.
4. Bring the water to a boil. Immediately pour the water into the flour mixture. Mix into a soft dough.
5. Use a paper towel dabbed with remaining butter to lightly grease the baking pan.
6. Divide the dough in half. Spoon half of the dough out of the bowl and pat it into the bottom of the baking pan.
7. Sprinkle 1 tablespoon (15 mL) of cornmeal over the dough.
8. Pour one can of gooseberries into the second bowl. With potato masher, crush the gooseberries into a pulp.
9. Stir in the other can of gooseberries, honey, and lemon juice.
10. Pour the gooseberry mixture over the layer of dough.
11. Top the gooseberry layer with the remaining dough. Sprinkle 1 tablespoon (15 mL) of cornmeal over the top.
12. Bake for 30 minutes, or until top is lightly browned.

Makes 6 servings

Sacagawea ran into the woods. Without looking back, she ran down a hill to the river, hoping to find a shallow place to cross. Sacagawea heard the voices of warriors and the sound of horses' hooves behind her. Many young women in her place might have thought it better to drown in the river than to be captured or killed by warriors.

Before the water reached her knees, Sacagawea heard the splashing of horse hooves. A Hidatsa warrior reached down and grabbed her. Sacagawea fought hard. She bit and scratched, but the warrior just laughed and held her firmly in front of him on the horse. As they rode through the forest back to the camp, Sacagawea could see the lifeless bodies of her people. Such a sight would surely have brought tears to the young woman's eyes.

Years after her capture, Sacagawea returned to the Jefferson River with the Lewis and Clark Expedition.

Back at the Lemhi Shoshone camp, Sacagawea saw her family's tepee blazing with fire. Near her tepee, Sacagawea noticed the dead body of her mother. Sacagawea turned her head away. It would have been difficult to hold back her sorrow any longer.

Sacagawea then saw Mountain Sage on the horse of another warrior. The sight of her dear friend may have been a comfort. Several of Sacagawea's other friends also had been captured by Hidatsa warriors.

The group of Hidatsa warriors and Lemhi Shoshone captives left the campsite. Before long, the smoke rising from the burning camp faded. Sacagawea certainly had fear about where the warriors were taking her and what would happen to her. Her Lemhi Shoshone life was behind her now. But Sacagawea surely hoped she would someday be reunited with her people.

CHAPTER 3

Living with the Hidatsa

Sacagawea lived in a dome-shaped earth lodge similar to the ones in this Hidatsa village.

Sacagawea, Mountain Sage, and another Lemhi Shoshone girl named Little Salmon, lived with one of the Hidatsa warriors who attacked their encampment. He lived in a large dome-shaped house made from timber, willow branches, grass, and clay. This earth lodge probably seemed strange to Sacagawea. Her family had always lived in tepees.

The Hidatsa women expected Sacagawea and her friends to work with them in the village. They learned how to plant gardens of squash and corn. Little Salmon did not like the village. She wanted to return to her people, the Lemhi Shoshone. Every day, she told Sacagawea and Mountain Sage that she planned to escape.

"I do not want to be a prisoner," Little Salmon told them. "I miss our people. You should escape with me." She promised that one night she would find the courage to run.

Sacagawea warned, "The way is long and dangerous. If they catch you, you will be punished." The thought of Little Salmon's punishment was enough to scare Sacagawea.

A few days later, Sacagawea awoke to the sound of many voices in the village. She heard one of the women say the Shoshone girl was gone. Sacagawea hurried out of her lodge to see if Little Salmon was the girl who had escaped. A Hidatsa woman walked up to Sacagawea. "Your friend is gone," she said. "What do you know about this?"

To avoid telling a lie, Sacagawea simply answered, "I know nothing." She then turned and went back into the lodge. Although afraid for her friend, Sacagawea hoped Little Salmon would make it safely across the plains to the Lemhi Shoshone people.

One evening, a French fur trader named Toussaint Charbonneau visited the Hidatsa warrior's lodge. The Frenchman had a lodge in the Hidatsa village. Charbonneau purchased Sacagawea and Mountain Sage from the Hidatsa warrior. They became his wives.

In October 1804, a group of white men were traveling near the Hidatsa village. Several Hidatsa men went to meet them. They learned that the white men were peaceful explorers with gifts for the Hidatsa chief. The Hidatsa men returned to the village with the group.

During the next two weeks, the explorers built a small camp several miles from the Hidatsa village. They called it Fort Mandan. Sacagawea noticed that Charbonneau made many trips to the white men's camp. After the white men finished building the camp, Charbonneau told Sacagawea to pack some supplies. They were going to live in the white men's village.

Sacagawea was nervous about moving into the strangers' camp. She would have a baby soon. She must have hoped Mountain Sage could help her when it was time for the baby's birth.

Sacagawea learned that the white men's names were Lewis and Clark. But she gave them different names. The one called Lewis carried a long knife with him at all times. Sacagawea called

Charbonneau (center), Sacagawea (holding buffalo skin), and Mountain Sage (by horse) brought gifts of buffalo skins to Lewis (left) and Clark (second from left).

him Big Knife. The first thing Sacagawea noticed about Clark was the color of his hair. She gave him the name Red Hair.

On February 11, 1805, Sacagawea felt the first pains of labor, signaling her baby's birth. All afternoon she struggled as the pains increased. Lewis ground and mixed two dried rings from a rattlesnake's tail with water. He gave this drink to Sacagawea.

"This medicine will help your pain and speed the birth of your baby," he told her. About 10 minutes after Sacagawea took the medicine, she gave birth to a baby boy. Charbonneau named the boy Jean Baptiste. But Sacagawea called him Pomp, which is a Lemhi Shoshone word meaning "child with lots of hair."

A month later, Charbonneau told Sacagawea they would be traveling west with the explorers. Sacagawea certainly would have been excited to see her family again. But she may also have been worried to make such a long, hard journey with a small baby.

CHAPTER 4
Traveling West

Sacagawea saw herds of buffalo on her journey west.

When the Missouri River thawed and water began to flow again, the white men decided to leave. Sacagawea hugged Mountain Sage. The two friends knew how much they would miss one another.

On April 7, 1805, Sacagawea, Pomp, Charbonneau, and the members of the Lewis and Clark Expedition started their journey to the Pacific Ocean. The group traveled both on land and on water. They took along six small canoes and two long and narrow sailboats called pirogues.

Sacagawea had never seen the strange long boats used for travel. She was used to riding on horseback. Traveling by horse was quicker than traveling by river. She did not understand why the explorers wanted to use boats.

Many of the things Red Hair and Big Knife owned and used surely puzzled Sacagawea. They spent much time using a compass. They seemed to use this

instrument to lead them. Sacagawea's people used the stars, sun, and moon to guide them. Each night, the white men wrote words on paper. Because they wrote every day, Sacagawea thought the papers must be very important.

On June 29, the group neared the Great Falls of the Missouri River. The sound of falling water was loud. Sacagawea could hear the falls a long distance away. When they neared the falls, the water rumbled so hard that the ground shook beneath their feet.

After exploring the area, Red Hair, Sacagawea, Pomp, and Charbonneau headed back to camp. The sky turned black and rain began to fall before they reached their camp. The rain fell so hard that the drops hurt Sacagawea's skin. They took shelter under a cliff overhang. Sacagawea set Pomp at her feet before lifting him out of his cradleboard.

Suddenly, water began rising on the ground where they stood, carrying away the cradleboard. Red Hair climbed up the rock to the top of the cliff and reached his hand to Sacagawea. She handed Pomp up to him. Sacagawea struggled to keep her footing as the water got higher. It flowed so strongly that she might have been swept away and into the river. Red Hair then helped Sacagawea and Charbonneau to safety.

A month later, the group camped near the Jefferson River. Sacagawea recognized the area as the exact spot where her people camped that fearful morning the Hidatsa warriors attacked her people. Sacagawea's memories of that day could have brought tears to her eyes. But she must have been comforted to know that she would soon see her Lemhi Shoshone people.

Sacagawea traveled a great distance with Pomp strapped to her back. When Sacagawea traveled with Lewis and Clark, she was much younger than the woman pictured in this painting.

Be an Interpreter

Sacagawea was an interpreter for Lewis and Clark. She could speak the Lemhi Shoshone language and understand the hand signs of other American Indian groups. Sacagawea would interpret the words and signs of American Indians into the Hidatsa language for Charbonneau. Charbonneau then translated the Hidatsa into French. Labiche, a member of the expedition, translated the French into English for Lewis and Clark. In this way, Lewis and Clark were able to communicate with native tribes during their journey. Try this simple interpreting exercise to help understand how the interpreters used different forms of communication to understand each other.

What You Do

1. Choose people to play these roles: American Indian stranger, Sacagawea, Charbonneau, Labiche, Lewis, and Clark.

2. The American Indian stranger makes up hand signs to communicate a simple message such as, "Eat lunch with me."

3. Out of the sight of the other players, the American Indian stranger signs his message to Sacagawea.

4. Sacagawea then whispers the message to Charbonneau so that the other players cannot hear her.

5. Charbonneau then draws a picture of the message he gets from Sacagawea to give to Labiche.

6. Labiche interprets the picture message and tells Lewis and Clark the American Indian's original message.

CHAPTER 5

Reunited with Cameahwait

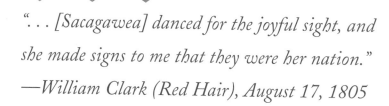

> ♦ ♦ ♦ ────────
>
> *". . . [Sacagawea] danced for the joyful sight, and she made signs to me that they were her nation."*
> —*William Clark (Red Hair), August 17, 1805*

On August 17, 1805, a small group of American Indian men rode on horseback toward the white men's group. Sacagawea recognized them as Lemhi Shoshone. She told Big Knife and Red Hair that these men were her people.

When the men came closer, Sacagawea shouted to them, "I am Sacagawea, the lost Lemhi Shoshone girl." She let the Lemhi Shoshone men know this group of travelers came in peace.

The men could have recognized Sacagawea as a Lemhi Shoshone from the designs painted on her forehead and upper cheek. The designs indicated she was from the Shoshone nation. The Shoshone invited the group to come to their camp.

Sacagawea was reunited with her people when the Lemhi Shoshone men took her to their camp.

When Sacagawea walked into the camp, many of the women ran to her. They asked Sacagawea many questions about her life. Sacagawea then saw the familiar face of Little Salmon. As soon as Sacagawea recognized Little Salmon, she ran to her, wrapping her arms around her friend. Both of the women cried as they hugged each other.

Sacagawea followed Red Hair and Big Knife into the council tent. She listened to the chief speak. Sacagawea recognized his voice. She looked him in the eyes. It was her brother, Cameahwait.

Red Hair purchased a horse for Sacagawea and Pomp to ride during their journey through the Bitterroot Mountains.

"Brother!" Sacagawea shouted. "Do you not know me? I am your sister, Sacagawea." She ran to him and wrapped her blanket shawl around the both of them. This act showed her love for him.

Charbonneau scolded Sacagawea for interrupting the council. He told her to sit down and translate. But Sacagawea could not stop crying. Big Knife saw that Sacagawea was overcome with happiness. He told the Lemhi Shoshone men that they could meet the next day.

After the men left the council tent, Sacagawea and her brother were alone. They hugged and cried. Sacagawea asked her brother about her family.

"Our father died shortly after the Hidatsa attack," Cameahwait replied. "He often worried about you, wondering if you were dead or alive. Our sister, Pine Girl, also died." Sacagawea cried at this news. Ever since the day she was taken prisoner, Sacagawea had hoped to see her family again someday.

Sacagawea told Cameahwait that the white men were mapping a trail traders could follow. The traders would bring guns, blankets, and beads to the Lemhi Shoshone. Sacagawea also explained that the white men wanted all tribes to be peaceful. In this way, all tribes could hunt and have enough food to feed their people. She tried to convince Cameahwait that it would be good for the Lemhi Shoshone people to give the white men horses to cross the mountains.

After 14 days with the Lemhi Shoshone people, Red Hair told Sacagawea that it was time to go. Sacagawea certainly was sad to say good-bye. Cameahwait asked her to stay. But Sacagawea told him that she must complete the journey. With 29 horses, three colts, and one mule, the group traveled into the Bitterroot Mountains. Red Hair gave Charbonneau items to trade for a horse for Sacagawea. It was a difficult journey.

CHAPTER 6
End of the Journey

Big Knife and Red Hair named Fort Clatsop after a local American Indian group. Clatsop Indians visited the group during their stay in Oregon.

On November 20, a Chinook man visited the group's camp. He was wearing a coat made from the skin of two otters. Red Hair and Big Knife tried to purchase the coat from the Chinook man, but the man refused to sell it.

Sacagawea saw how much the white men wanted the coat. She took off the blue-beaded belt she wore around her waist. She offered it to the Chinook man. He accepted the trade and gave the coat to Red Hair. Red Hair was so grateful that he later gave Sacagawea a coat made of blue cloth.

By December, the group reached the Oregon coast. They were only a few miles from the Pacific coast. They built a winter village and called it Fort Clatsop.

On Christmas Day, Sacagawea and Charbonneau joined Red Hair, Big Knife, and the other men for a celebration. Sacagawea gave Red Hair a valuable gift of two dozen white weasel tails to decorate his otter-skin coat. The gift was meant to thank him for being so kind to Pomp throughout the journey. Little Salmon had once given Sacagawea these weasel tails as a gift.

The following spring, Sacagawea traveled back to the Hidatsa village with Red Hair and Big Knife. On August 17, 1806, Sacagawea once again stepped into an earth lodge. Sacagawea told Mountain Sage about the long journey. She talked about the dangers they experienced and the visit with their Lemhi Shoshone people. As Mountain Sage listened, Sacagawea also told about Cameahwait and her family.

Red Hair wanted to take Pomp to live with him. He offered to send Pomp to school. Sacagawea thought it would be best to wait until Pomp was older. Charbonneau told Red Hair that they would bring Pomp to him when the boy grew older.

In 1809, Sacagawea and Charbonneau traveled with Pomp to St. Louis, Missouri. There, Charbonneau bought farmland from Red Hair. Missing their traditional way of life, Charbonneau and Sacagawea decided to return to the plains in 1811. They left Pomp to live with Red Hair. They then traveled to Fort Manuel in present-day South Dakota, where Charbonneau had taken a job as a trader.

In 1812, Sacagawea had a daughter, Lisette. After the birth of her daughter, Sacagawea became ill with a fever. On December 20, 1812, Sacagawea died at Fort Manuel. She was 24 years old.

Sacagawea's son, Pomp, was a year-and-a-half old when they returned to the Hidatsa village.

Chronology

April 7, 1805
Sacagawea begins her journey with the Lewis and Clark Expedition.

December 1805
Sacagawea and the Lewis and Clark Expedition reach the Oregon coast. They build Fort Clatsop.

1800
Sacagawea's Lemhi Shoshone camp is attacked by Hidatsa warriors. Sacagawea is taken captive.

August 1806
Sacagawea returns to the Hidatsa village.

1788
Sacagawea is born.

August 1805
Sacagawea is reunited with her brother, Cameahwait.

December 20, 1812
Sacagawea dies at Fort Manuel in present-day South Dakota.

February 11, 1805
Sacagawea gives birth to Pomp at Fort Mandan.

1809
Sacagawea and Charbonneau take Pomp to St. Louis, Missouri, to live with Clark.

Words to Know

annual (AN-yoo-uhl)—happening once a year

burden (BUR-duhn)—a heavy load, either physical or emotional

compass (KUHM-puhss)—a navigating instrument used to find directions

expedition (ek-spuh-DISH-uhn)—a long journey for a certain purpose, such as exploring

interpreter (in-TUR-prit-uhr)—someone who can tell others what is said in another language

native (NAY-tiv)—people who originally lived in a particular place or area; American Indians were natives of North America.

nomadic (noh-MA-dik)—a way of life that involves traveling from place to place

overcome (oh-vur-KUHM)—to experience to such a great degree that one is helpless because of it; Sacagawea was overcome with emotion when she saw her brother.

overhang (oh-vur-HANG)—an area or part of land that extends over the ground to create a shelter

warrior (WOR-ee-ur)—a person who fights in battle

To Learn More

Bruchac, Joseph. *Sacajawea: The Story of Bird Woman and the Lewis and Clark Expedition.* San Diego: Silver Whistle, 2000.

Gleiter, Jan, and Kathleen Thompson. *Sacagawea.* First Biographies. Austin, Texas: Raintree Steck-Vaughn, 1995.

Roop, Peter, and Connie Roop. *Girl of the Shining Mountains: Sacagawea's Story.* New York: Hyperion Books, 1999.

Thomasma, Kenneth. *The Truth about Sacajawea.* Jackson, Wyo.: Grandview Publishing, 1997.

Tinling, Marion. *Sacagawea's Son: The Story of Jean Baptiste Charbonneau.* Missoula, Mont.: Mountain Press Publishing, 2001.

Witteman, Barbara. *Sacagawea: A Photo-Illustrated Biography.* Photo-Illustrated Biographies. Mankato, Minn.: Bridgestone Books, 2002.

Internet Sites

Discovering Lewis and Clark
http://www.lewis-clark.org

Hero History: Sacagawea
http://www.imahero.com/herohistory/sacagawea_herohistory.htm

Lewis and Clark: The Journey of the Corps of Discovery
http://www.pbs.org/lewisandclark

Pomp: The True Story of the Baby on the Sacagawea Dollar, an E-book for Kids
http://pompstory.home.mindspring.com

Places to Visit

Lewis and Clark Interpretive Center and Fort Mandan
P.O. Box 607
U.S. Hwy 83 and North Dakota Hwy 200A
Washburn, ND 58577–0607

Lewis and Clark Interpretive Center and the Plains Indians
4201 Giant Springs Road
P.O. Box 1806
Great Falls, MT 59403-1806

Museum of Westward Expansion
Jefferson National Expansion Memorial
11 North Fourth Street
St. Louis, MO 63102

Sacajawea State Park & Interpretive Center
2503 Sacajawea Park Road
Pasco, WA 99301

Index